MISSION
ST. AUGUSTINE

Creator: Catherine Aragon
Cover Designer: Nada Orlić - Skyline Designer: Manjinder Singh

www.ScavengerHuntAdventures.com

MISSION LOCATION

ST. AUGUSTINE

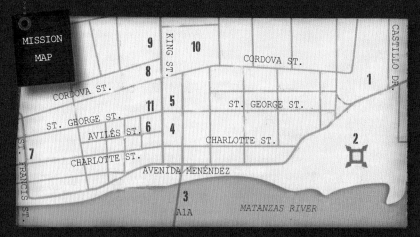

MISSION MAP

9
KING ST.
10
CORDOVA ST.
1
CASTILLO DR.
8
CORDOVA ST.
11
5
ST. GEORGE ST.
ST. GEORGE ST.
6
AVILÉS ST.
4
CHARLOTTE ST.
2
7
CHARLOTTE ST.
ST. FRANCIS ST.
AVENIDA MENÉNDEZ
3
A1A
MATANZAS RIVER

ST. AUGUSTINE HISTORIC DISTRICT

CONTENTS:

MISSION NUMBER		MISSION NAME	PAGE NUMBER	POINT VALUE	MY POINTS
	■	Mission Information	2		
	■	Mission Rules	3		
1	■	Visitor Center	4	22	
2	■	Castillo San Marcos	10	23	
3	■	Bridge of Lions	16	6	
4	■	Plaza de la Constitución	18	37	
5	■	Government House	28	12	
6	■	Avilés Street	32	22	
7	■	Oldest House	36	15	
8	■	Lightner Museum Square	40	25	
9	■	Zorayda Castle	44	9	
10	■	Flagler College	48	25	
11	■	St. George Street	52	47	
12	■	Anytime Missions	58	81	
		Answer Key	60		
		The Final Mission	61		

AFTER COMPLETING EACH MISSION, CHECK (√) THE BOX AND WRITE THE NUMBER OF POINTS EARNED.

AT THE END, WRITE THE TOTAL NUMBER OF POINTS HERE:

SEE MAP ON THE OTHER PAGE FOR MISSION LOCATIONS.

1

ATTENTION: FUTURE SPECIAL AGENTS <u>YOU</u> AND <u>CASE OFFICERS</u>

....

CONGRATULATIONS! THE SIA (SECRET INTERNATIONAL AGENCY) HAS SELECTED YOU AS A CANDIDATE TO BECOME A SPECIAL AGENT.

The SIA carries out important assignments, secretly collecting intelligence in all corners of the globe. ("Intelligence" is spy-speak for "information.") Currently, we are in dire need of agents. Many want to join us, but only a few have what it takes.

HOW WILL YOU PROVE YOU'RE READY TO JOIN THE MOST ELITE SPY AGENCY IN THE WORLD? You must complete a series of missions in St. Augustine. Similar to a scavenger hunt (only better), these missions will require you to carry out challenging investigations and collect valuable intel (short for "intelligence"). For each mission, you'll earn points towards becoming a special agent.

YOUR ASSIGNMENT: TRAVEL TO ST. AUGUSTINE WITH YOUR TEAM, LED BY YOUR CASE OFFICER. Your team will need to decide on a case officer (i.e., an adult). You must earn at least 200 points to become a special agent.

1- This is (mostly) an outdoor hunt. No need to worry about attraction closing times (or admission fees). Just make sure you're done before dark!

2- The mission list and mission scorecard are on page 1. All missions are in the central Historic District. If you need a map, it's opposite page 1.

3- You don't need to complete all the missions to earn 200 points or complete them in any certain order.

4- Scan the pages of each mission before starting to be fully prepared.

5- Read the "Anytime Missions" early, so that you'll remain on alert and ready to earn points. You can complete these at any time during the hunt.

6- Bring a pen/pencil and a camera.

MISSION RULES

- Be kind and respectful to team members.

- Your case officer has the final decision regarding point awards.

- Your case officer serves as the official "scorekeeper."

- Your case officer has the final decision on what missions will be attempted. (Don't worry, you can still earn enough points to become an agent without completing all the missions.)

- Always be on alert. You never know when a chance to earn points lies just around the corner.

TO CONCEAL THEIR REAL IDENTITIES, SPECIAL AGENTS ALWAYS USE CODE NAMES. FOR EXAMPLE, JAMES BOND'S CODE NAME IS 007. THINK OF YOUR OWN CODE NAME TO USE DURING YOUR MISSION IN ST. AUGUSTINE.

SIGN YOUR CODE NAME HERE:

Agent Leona

———————————

DATE

LET THE MISSIONS BEGIN - GOOD LUCK!

VISITOR CENTER

AGENTS MUST HAVE TOP-NOTCH SKILLS IN IMAGE ANALYSIS. FREQUENTLY YOU'LL HAVE TO ANALYZE IMAGES, SEARCHING FOR VALUABLE CLUES. TIME TO PUT YOUR SKILLS TO THE TEST!

Hunt down these "masks," replicas of the centuries-old originals (which also spout water) in St. Augustine's "Sister City." The image above has the faces out of order. Compare these faces to the faces at the Visitor's Center.

☐ **WHAT'S THE CORRECT ORDER OF THE FACES?**

4 POINTS

22

TOTAL POINTS

- 'MASKS' ORDER
- SISTER CITIES
- OLD SPANISH TRAIL
- SANCHEZ-SOLANA SIGN
- MATANZAS
- YELLOW JACK

For the next two pieces of "intel," read the fountain sign.

☐ WHAT'S THE NAME OF ST. AUGUSTINE'S SISTER CITY?

2
POINTS

As "Sister Cities" St. Augustine and this city exchange gifts. One of St. Augustine's gifts: an item from a 1600's treasure ship, the *Atocha* ("*Uh-toe-chah*"), whose loot remained missing off the Florida Keys for almost 400 years.

THE STORY OF THE ATOCHA

The year 1622 spelled **D-I-S-A-S-T-E-R** for the Spanish treasure fleet. Laden with gold, silver, and gems from the Americas, the fleet with the *Atocha* set off from Cuba back to Spain - in the midst of hurricane season. Not so smart. In the Florida Keys, sure enough, a fierce hurricane sent the *Atocha* to the bottom of the sea and drowned most of her crew.

Spanish ships in Havana, Cuba

5

Spanish ships in Havana, Cuba

The Spanish were desperate to locate the lost treasure ships. **Spain needed the loot ASAP** to pay for war back in Europe.

To recover shipwrecks the Spanish sent slaves diving deep, sometimes **luring them to make these death-wish dives with the promise of freedom** to the one who could locate a wreck and bring back a bar of silver. Between the 1500's and 1700's these divers recovered enough loot to save Spain from going bankrupt.

Unfortunately for the divers (and for Spain) **the _Atocha_ treasure remained lost for hundreds of years.** Finally in 1985, an American team led by treasure hunter Mel Fisher uncovered it. After a grueling 16-year search (that included the

Spanish Gold & Silver

drowning death of Fisher's son), the team found the **"Atocha Mother Lode": a $450 million bounty.** Fisher's team thought they'd struck gold, but government officials said **not so fast.** The battle went all the way to the U.S. Supreme Court. The Court ruled in favor of Fisher's team. **Finders keepers.**

☐ **WHAT ITEM FROM THE ATOCHA DID ST. AUGUSTINE GIVE TO ITS SISTER CITY?**

2 POINTS

Sánchez

Solana

Find the marker for the "Zero Milestone Marker of the Old Spanish Trail," an auto trail that once linked old Spanish settlements.

☐ THE TRAIL ENDED IN WHICH CITY?

2 POINTS

The Spanish settled this city, and the original Spanish name stuck. Even though the Spanish settled St. Augustine, today we call the city by its English name.

☐ ST. AUGUSTINE'S SPANISH NAME WAS:

2 POINTS

S __AN__ A __gustin__.

For the answer to this clue and for the clue on the next page...

☐ FIND A SIGN WITH THESE TWO COATS-OF-ARMS.

2 POINTS

St. Augustine, 1763: 3,100 people – gone. They packed up everything and skipped town (most of them, except for a few families, like the ones of these coats-of-arms). They hopped on boats to sail down the coast and to start anew on an island.

St. Augustine

☐ **TO WHAT ISLAND DID CITY RESIDENTS GO?**

That year, 1763, Spain lost Florida to its arch-rival Britain. Spain would get its revenge down the road, helping 13 colonies defeat the all-mighty British Empire in our war for independence.

☐ **FIND THE NAME OF THE CITY'S MATANZAS RIVER IN LETTERS MADE OF TINY STONES.**

This river gets its name from a not-so-pleasant Spanish word. Matanzas = "Slaughters."

THE STORY OF THE "MATANZAS"

Menéndez

When Pedro Menéndez arrived here in 1565, he came with an order from the Spanish king: **do away with the French - by any means necessary.** The French had been bold enough to settle on lands claimed by Spain (Florida). Thanks to a **spy**, the king knew of France's plans to make Ft. Caroline (their settlement) even bigger. **The agent even managed to get intel directly from expedition leader Jean Ribault** (*"Jhah Ree-bo"*) **himself.**

On September 4 the Spanish and French fleets crossed paths, but the real drama wouldn't unfold until later that month and into

Ribault

October, beginning with **a violent storm that changed history.**

Ribault was on the hunt for Menéndez, but the storm shipwrecked him, and left Menéndez to take the French fort north of St.

Augustine. Ribault's crew came ashore, divided up, and soon began a long march to return to their fort – **BIG MISTAKE.** Menéndez tracked the crew down south of St. Augustine. Most of them met their end at the blood-thirsty blades of Spanish weapons. And today, Ribault's ship remains still lost on the ocean floor.

Around the corner from the Visitor Center (towards the Castillo)

☐ **LOCATE THIS TRIANGLE DESIGN. IT STANDS ABOVE A CEMETERY BUILT TO BURY VICTIMS OF WHICH DISEASE?**

3 POINTS

Horrible pain, chills, and eyes with a tell-tale yellow tint – these were symptoms of **a deadly disease that called on St. Augustine in 1821.**

When the city built this cemetery, people thought it was transmitted person to person (like a cold). **The city closed to all outsiders.** The only relief – the arrival of cool weather that took care of the infected mosquitoes, the true culprit.

(Don't worry, today the disease affects tropical areas of Africa & South America – and there are vaccines to protect us.)

CASTILLO SAN MARCOS

(Castillo = "Kah-stee-oh")

ONE OF THE TOP RULES OF SPYING: BLEND IN WITH YOUR SURROUNDINGS. YOU CAN NEVER SPOT THE BEST AGENTS, BECAUSE THEY DON'T *LOOK* LIKE AGENTS. HERE, THAT MEANS "PLAYING TOURIST" BY STROLLING AROUND AN OLD FORTRESS.

☐ **FROM THE CASTILLO, SPOT THIS CROSS.**

2
POINTS

It towers over the site of "Nombre de Dios" (*"Nohm-bray Day Dee-ohs"*) ("Name of God") and may also protect the city from hurricanes. Since construction in the 1960's, a major hurricane hasn't hit the city.

23

- GIANT CROSS
- WATCHTOWER
- DEFENSE SYSTEM
- FADED 'NEW SPAIN' COLORS
- CANNONS
- SPAIN COAT-OF-ARMS

TOTAL POINTS

This place, together with the next-door Fountain of Youth Park, marks the spot where Pedro Menéndez, the city's founder, landed.

Timucuans

At your next Thanksgiving, think about this spot, as St. Augustine lays claim to the first "Thanksgiving." No feasting on turkey back then. It was beans, bread, and salted meats. The Menéndez crew shared the meal with the Native Americans (the Timucuans) whose village

they landed upon, and the Spanish pastor led a ceremony giving thanks to God for a safe arrival. The Spanish couldn't have made it here without the Timucua, who gave them shelter and knew these parts like the backs of their hands.

☐ FIND THE COLONIAL QUARTER'S WOODEN WATCHTOWER.

1 POINT

In 1586 a watchtower stood tall watching over the land and sea. Built to alert townspeople for enemies on the horizon, it actually ended up giving away St. Augustine's location to the fierce pirate, Francis Drake (a.k.a. "The Dragon").

Drake

Drake's Raid

To the English, Francis Drake was a brave seafarer who explored the world, sailing the seas for the English crown. However, **to the Spanish, "The Dragon" was a dreadful pirate who terrorized their ships and ports.**

In June of 1586, Drake's 2,300-strong crew stormed on to St. Augustine. **They set the town ablaze, and sent the townspeople fleeing for their lives.**

St. Augustine was a poor, middle-of-nowhere military town, without the riches of Spain's other colonies like Puerto Rico ("Rich Port") or Mexico. No mighty fortress guarded the city…yet.

In May of 1668 another pirate (Robert Searle) snuck into St. Augustine under the dark of night and raided the town.

With the treasury's silver looted, residents sent to their deaths, and the town invaded (again), the ruler Mariana of Spain knew something had to be done. Finally, in 1672, construction began on the Castillo with coquina ("*ko-kee-nah*") (shell stone).

Mariana

The coquina fortress saved St. Augustine from the British. British guns could do serious damage to brick or granite, but **not even cannonballs could take down the coquina of the Castillo.**

Castillo = castle, but the Spanish didn't build this as a palace for a king or queen. (No royal ever left Spain to visit the colonies.) Back then it was about pure military strategy.

LOCATE THESE ITEMS, KEY TO THE CASTILLO DEFENSE SYSTEM (ONE POINT EACH):

1 POINT EACH

☐ **THE SINGLE ENTRANCE:** One way in and one way out: keep enemies out and protect those inside

☐ **DRAWBRIDGE**

☐ **MOAT:** Meant to remain dry to hold livestock (a.k.a. fresh meat for food during a siege); If enemies attacked over land, the moat could fill with sea water for a **short** time. Years ago water sat...and sat...and sat in the moat (like this postcard). Big mistake - the water began to crack the coquina.

The Oldest City in the United States

☐ **GLACIS:** Open, sloped greens around the fortress made approaching enemies easy targets

☐ **RAVELIN:** A triangle-shaped "island" to protect the fortress entrance

• •

The Spanish finished off the fort with the colors of New Spain using plaster the colors of red (now faded on the sentry boxes) and white (on the walls). Some of this remains today, although the red is harder to spot.

☐ **LOCATE THE FADED RED AND WHITE.**

3 POINTS

Flag of New Spain (Spanish colonies in North America, Caribbean Islands, and the Philippines)

13

☐ **ONE POINT FOR EVERY CANNON SPOTTED.**
10 POINTS MAX

☐ **FIND THE REMAINS OF**
THIS COAT-OF-ARMS.

The crest once appeared like
this image, but time has worn
away the crest you'll find.
Try to make out the remains of
the two lions and two castles.
They represent two regions
of Spain: León ("Lion") and
Castilla ("Land of Castles").
*(León = "Lay-ohn"; Castilla =
"Kah-stee-ah")*

my notes:

_____

_____

_____

CASTILLO PRISONER: OSCEOLA

One of the castillo's most famous prisoners: the great Seminole leader Osceola (*"Oh-see-oh-luh"*).

When the U.S. took control of Florida they wanted the Seminoles out. The two sides waged war and **in the 1830's Osceola rallied his people to fight**. Time and time again the U.S. had the Seminoles sign unfair treaties forcing them off their homelands.

While no angel himself, **Osceola was well respected by even his enemy** (the U.S.) for his smarts and his leadership. The only way the U.S. managed to bring him down: a general tricked him into meeting, under the cover of a truce, and then captured him. They threw him into the Castillo, but then transferred him to South Carolina where the great leader sadly died as a prisoner.

> Osceola's response to this treaty: stab it with a knife.

Seminoles = Comes from the Spanish word "Cimarrón" ("see-mar-ohn"*) = "runaway." Seminoles came from other Native American tribes who had "run away" to escape in Florida. Here, they were joined by runaway slaves who became known as "Black Seminoles." In the 1800's the Seminoles put up a long, hard fight against the U.S. to try to stay in Florida.

BRIDGE OF LIONS

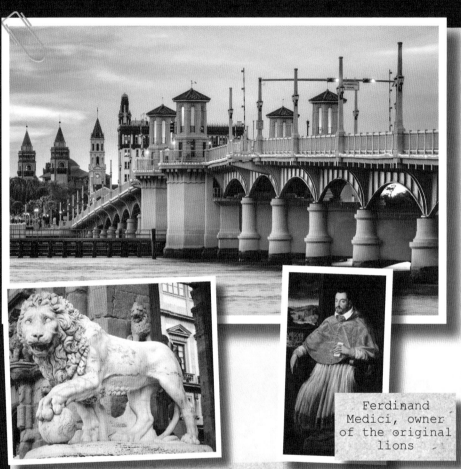

Ferdinand Medici, owner of the original lions

Original lion in Florence, Italy

The "Medici" (*Meh-dee-chee*) lions, named after the powerful Medici family of Italy, guard this bridge. These lions are replicas of those which once guarded a Medici palace.

6

- LION STATUES
- BRIDGE OPENING
- HAUNTED LIGHTHOUSE

☐ **HAVE YOUR PHOTO TAKEN UNDER ONE OF THE LIONS.** **2** POINTS

Better not be in a hurry while crossing this bridge. This drawbridge lifts its "leaves" for passing vessels - and you may get caught on the bridge as it lifts and lowers.

☐ **BONUS: BEFORE LEAVING TOWN, SEE (OR HEAR) THE BRIDGE OF LIONS OPEN.** **2** POINTS
(It will sound like a fog horn.)

☐ **FIND ST. AUGUSTINE'S LIGHTHOUSE ON THE HORIZON.** **2** POINTS

St. Augustine's Lighthouse (**a.k.a. the most haunted place in town**) has stood on Anastasia Island since 1874. The reported spirits:

#1: Joseph Andreu, the keeper who fell to his death in 1859 while painting the earlier lighthouse. He still mills about keeping watch over the tower.

#2: Three girls who drowned at the lighthouse in 1873 when they were playing in a construction cart. The card slid off its path and landed in the water below. Their laughs still echo through the lighthouse.

PLAZA DE LA CONSTITUCIÓN

("Plaza deh lah Con-stee-tu-see-ohn")

Catholic Cathedral and Plaza, St. Augustine, Florida

67376

1930's

1850's

Plaza dela Constitution.

SPECIAL AGENTS MUST ALWAYS HAVE THEIR EYES PEELED FOR INTELLIGENCE: CLUES AND CRITICAL INFO THAT OTHERS OFTEN OVERLOOK. CAN YOU FIND THE 'INTEL' NEEDED TO COMPLETE THIS MISSION?

☐ **FIND FOUR INSCRIPTIONS LIKE THIS, WITH "PLAZA DE LA CONSTITUCION."**

4 POINTS

Plaza de la Constitución = Constitution Plaza (in case you didn't guess). Here stands one of the only monuments in the world to Spain's "constitution that never was."

37

TOTAL POINTS

- PLAZA INSCRIPTION
- POW'S DOCUMENT
- FLAGPOLE FACES
- PONCE STATUE
- FLORIDA TRIVIA
- WOOLWORTH'S

- PLAZA PROTESTORS
- CIVIL RIGHTS QUOTES
- LATITUDE/LONGITUDE
- POPE CREST
- U.S. SEAL

The year was 1812, and a French emperor named Napoleon controlled much of Spain. Despite French control, a Spanish assembly managed to break away and create a new constitution. **All of Spain (including St. Augustine) got orders to put up new "constitution" monuments.**

Napoleon

Spain soon managed to say "adiós" to the French and the royal family came back to power. Then, Spain's king Ferdinand VII (VII=7), sometimes called **the worst Spanish king in history**, did away with the constitution and **ordered the constitution monuments destroyed.**

Ferdinand

St. Augustine had spent way too much to build the constitution monument. **The last thing they'd do: tear it down.** And here it remains.

Constitution Banner: The Lion (Spain) attacks the eagle (France); Constitución Española = Spanish Constitution

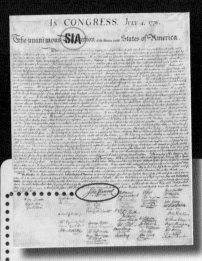

During the Revolutionary War, the city remained with the British, who held patriots as POWs (Prisoners of War), including three signers of one of our most important documents.

☐ WHAT DOCUMENT DID THESE POWS SIGN?

2 POINTS

Hint: Find a Prisoners of War sign for this intel.

Unlike the colonies to the north, Florida did not want to join the soon-to-be United States. These Loyalists (so-called for their loyalty to Britain) had too many ties to Britain. The Loyalist response to the document you just found: city residents created life-like dolls (called "effigies") of Founding Fathers John Hancock and John Adams. **Then, they took to the streets for a public "hanging" of Hancock and Adams in protest.**

Hancock; first to sign your clue's document

Adams; 2nd President

1

2

3

4

5

6

These six faces lie just off the plaza. Each of them represents a different period of St. Augstine's history, with an important year inscribed above each face.

☐ **TRACK DOWN THESE SIX FACES.**

5
POINTS

Hint: Look for a cannon, cannonballs, and a flagpole.

my notes:

21

Diego

Ponce

Bartholomew

Find the statue of Ponce de León near the plaza.

☐ **HAVE YOUR PHOTO SNAPPED, POSING LIKE PONCE.**

3 POINTS

Legend has it Juan Ponce de León (*"Wahn Ponce deh Lay-ohn"*) arrived here in search of the **magical Fountain of Youth** – waters that made the old young again and cured disease. No one found the magical fountain - and Ponce died in 1521, from an Indian arrow.

After battling the Moors in Spain (see p.45), Ponce sailed with Christopher Columbus on his second voyage in 1493. Soon though, **Ponce's arch-rival was none other than Columbus' power-hungry son, Diego.** Diego wanted to milk the "Columbus" name for all it was worth and have another Columbus (Bartholomew) sail instead to search for more territory. **Ponce, though, beat out the Columbus crew to get the king's OK.**

☐ **WHAT YEAR DID PONCE LAND IN FLORIDA?**

1 POINT

Ponce claimed the land, naming it after Spain's "Pascua Florida," the Easter Festival of Flowers. Some say he landed a bit north of St. Augustine, others say much further south (at Melbourne Beach). Our vote - the spot near St. Augustine!

Track down a plaque with this seal for the next three clues.

☐ **WHAT YEAR DID THE U.S. ACQUIRE FLORIDA?**

In the early 1800's the U.S. had its eye on Florida – another territory to add to the growing United States.

Jackson

Does the name "Jacksonville" sound familiar? The city up the road is named for **Andrew Jackson,** the general (and future president) who **would stop at nothing to claim Florida from Spain.** He ignored orders and invaded Florida to attack the Spanish. He did everything he could to push out the Native Americans (the Seminoles) and stomp out any remaining British desire to claim Florida.

Spain realized the U.S. was going to take Florida one way or another, and **best to avoid the wrath of Andrew Jackson.** The two nations made a deal, and Florida became part of the United States.

☐ **WHAT YEAR DID FLORIDA BECOME A STATE?**

☐ **WHAT IS THE STATE SONG?**

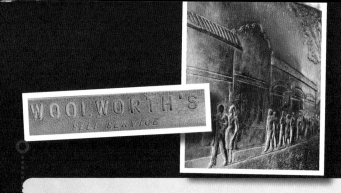

☐ **FIND THE OLD DOOR HANDLES, REMAINS FROM THE "WOOLWORTH'S" DINER.** *3 POINTS*

Here in 1963 the "St. Augustine Four," four African-American teens, were arrested. **Their crime: trying to order soda and a burger at the whites-only lunch counter.**

St. Augustine played a major role in getting the Civil Rights Act passed, an act that outlawed discrimination against someone based on race, gender, or religion.

☐ **FIND THE ABOVE TWO IMAGES OF THE PLAZA.** *2 POINTS*

This sculpture shows Americans who fought for equality. Protesters not only marched, but were sometimes arrested, beaten, and shot at. In 1963, Dr. Robert Hayling (the "Father of the St. Augustine Movement") led a group of 100 African Americans to protest, with police arresting a quarter of them.

King at a Civil Rights rally

By 1964, the city reached a boiling point. Martin Luther King, Jr. called on college students to skip the usual Spring Break beach vacations in Florida and come instead to protest. Even the 72-year-old mother of the Massachusetts governor came to protest – and was thrown in jail.

Young

Dr. King, Pres. Johnson, and Civil Rights leaders

One night protesters arrived, led by a man named Andrew Young, and the racist group that awaited beat him. Following the message of non-violence preached by King, **the group responded by simply walking away.**

☐ **WHAT DATE WAS THIS "MARCH TO THE PLAZA?"** **2** POINTS
Hint: Find a plaque containing a photo of Young.

Young, who also led protests in Selma, Alabama (heard of the movie *Selma*?). He'd go on to serve as a congressman, mayor, and our representative to the United Nations.

WHO SPOKE THE QUOTES BELOW? **3** POINTS
Hint: Keep a lookout below your feet.

~~Events in St.~~ **Augustine** (and around the country) **finally pushed the act through Congress.** The president in the photo above signed the Civil Rights Act into law on July 2, 1964.

☐ "St. Augustine was probably the most rigorous test that non-violence had. And we passed it. If we had not passed it, we could have lost the Civil Rights Act."

☐ "We have allowed the idea of non-violence to work through us and transform dark yesterdays into bright tomorrows."

☐ "The Civil Rights Act is a challenge to all of us to eliminate the last vestiges* of injustice in our beloved country."

*vestige = trace

In the plaza stand memorials to St. Augustine residents who gave their lives in war. While exploring, take a moment to remember those that gave their lives in military service.

SPECIAL AGENTS MUST HAVE EXCELLENT MAP-READING ABILITIES.

St. Augustine's exact location on a map:

_____ DEGREES NORTH, _____ DEGREES WEST

☐ **WHAT ARE THE TWO DIGIT NUMBERS FOR THE LATITUDE AND LONGITUDE?**

3
POINTS

Hint: Examine the outside of the plaza's buildings for this intel.

my notes:

☐ **FIND THE GREAT SEAL OF THE UNITED STATES ON THE OUTSIDE OF A BUILDING.**

3 POINTS

Here, the eagle spreads its wings while holding 13 arrows in its left talon (symbolizing the 13 original states) and an olive branch in its right talon (symbolizing peace). Together, they show that the while the U.S. prefers peace (the eagle faces the olive branch), the nation is always ready for war.

☐ **LOCATE THE SYMBOL OF THE POPE, THE LEADER OF THE CATHOLIC CHURCH.**

3 POINTS

At the top: the crown of the Pope surrounded by keys.

The current Pope: Pope Francis

GOVERNMENT HOUSE

1930's

ALL THE SPY GEAR AND TOP SECRET INTEL IN THE WORLD WON'T HELP YOU IF YOU DON'T HAVE SHARP EYES AND A MIND LIKE A STEEL TRAP. LET'S TEST YOUR SKILLS ON THE GROUNDS OF THIS MONUMENT.

Since 1598 a government building (of some sort) has stood here: capitol building, governor's house, courthouse, and hospital. In the 1930's it served as a customs house and _____ _____.

☐ **WHAT WAS THIS FUNCTION?** **2** POINTS

Hint: Find an inscription dated 1935. Look at the title of the second person.

12

TOTAL POINTS

In April 2001, the *former* King and Queen of Spain greeted St. Augustine from the building's balcony.

☐ **WHAT ARE THEIR NAMES?** **2** POINTS

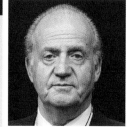

the mystery king

Hint: Find a brown bronze plaque for this intel.

We put "former" in *italics* because this king and queen stepped down in 2014, and their son, Felipe (*"Fay-lee-pay"*) and Felipe's wife, Letizia (*"Lay-tiz-ee-a"*), took over the crown. Rumor has it they'll attend St. Augustine's 450th birthday celebration in September, 2015.

the mystery queen

my notes:

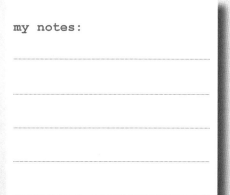

Felipe & Letizia

Ismail the Magnificent

☐ **FIND A VERSION OF THIS FLAG, A FORMER FLAG OF EGYPT.** (With three crescents, three stars)

2 POINTS

•••••••• **DON'T READ ON UNTIL YOU FIND THE FLAG.** ••••••••

☐ **HOW MANY STARS DOES THE AMERICAN FLAG ON THIS MONUMENT HAVE?**

2 POINTS

When the Civil War broke out in 1861, the nation had this many states.

Loring (left arm lost in Mexican American War)

The story of the Egyptian flag starts at the end of the 1800's. The leader, Ismail the Magnificent, wanted to modernize his military. So, he turned to American military leaders like William Loring who fought in history's "First Modern War" – the Civil War – where the North (Union) battled the South (Confederacy). (Florida – and Loring – had joined the Confederacy.)

What made the Civil War the "First Modern War":

- **The Train:** Delivered troops & supplies way faster than horses

- **Aerial Intel:** Balloons floated up in the sky so passengers could gather valuable intel on the enemy and make battle plans

Aerial Intel

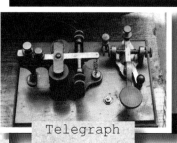
Telegraph

Ironclads

- **The Telegraph:** Old-fashioned text messaging; No need to wait on messengers on horseback - info was delivered via Morse Code (a series of dots and dashes) thanks to electric signals sent through wires.

- **Iron Clad Ships:** Adiós to weak wooden vessels

For his service in Egypt, Loring achieved the rank of "Pasha" (Egyptian general).

Loring - The Pasha

☐ **TRACK DOWN THIS MARKER.**

2 POINTS

"Rosario" (Spanish for "rosary") = a necklace with a handful of beads. The Rosario section of the old city wall was the "necklace" and the beads were the "redoubts" (a.k.a. mini-forts).

The location of the street next to the above marker was once the city's border.

☐ **WHAT BORDER WAS IT?** (NORTH/SOUTH/EAST/WEST)

2 POINTS

Hint: Locate a sign with a crest of two lions and two castles, like the image on p.14.

AVILÉS STREET

("Ah-vee-lays")

Begin where Avilés Street meets the Plaza.

Beneath the bricks you walk across, under the
ground, lie the remains of the oldest street in
the U.S...and one of the nation's most haunted.
Let's start with an easy clue.

☐ **FIND THIS VERSION OF THE AVILÉS COAT-OF-
ARMS.**

In case you haven't heard already, Avilés is the
home of St. Augustine's founder Pedro Menéndez.

In colonial times residents didn't call this
street "Avilés."

☐ **WHAT WAS THIS STREET'S NAME (IN ENGLISH)?**

Hint: The answer lies by the street's entrance.

- COATS-OF-ARMS
- CHURCH IMAGE
- HAUNTED BUILDING COAT-OF-ARMS
- STATUES
- 1800'S PHOTO
- 2004 MOVIE
- NUNS' SYMBOL

The Spanish built the church of "Nuestra Señora de los Remedios" ("*Nway-stra Sen-yora deh los Reh-meh-dee-ose*") near the entrance. Buildings line Avilés Street now. However, in colonial times **the church cemetery lay here, filled with bodies of those who met their end at the hands of St. Augustine's rough and tumble frontier life**: dying from the likes of disease, hunger, and pirate raids. Their souls may live on, haunting Avilés Street today.

····This old painting shows the 1586 raid of the pirate Francis Drake (see p.12 for more on the raid). Time to test your image analysis skills. Note the location of the water on the painting. Then, look at where Avilés Street lies today in relation to the water. Next, examine the image for tiny, faded black letters.

Circle the church of Nuestra Señora on the painting, marked with a faded letter "O."

☐ **FIND THE SAME PAINTING DISPLAYED ON THE STREET TO CHECK YOUR ANSWER. (THE CHURCH WILL BE CIRCLED IN RED.)**

3
POINTS

☐ **HUNT DOWN THIS DESIGN.**

2
POINTS

This coat-of-arms lies on a building reported to be haunted by soldiers who died inside its walls.

33

☐ **FIND THESE TWO COATS-OF-ARMS PAINTED ON TILES.** (Left: St. Augustine; Right: Avilés)

4 POINTS

☐ **FIND STATUES OF TWO MEN FACING EACH OTHER.**

2 POINTS

In this sculpture, in a courtyard just off the street, a bag rests at the feet of one man, and the other man wears a college robe. **Both men were born in the house that surrounds the courtyard: one was enslaved, one was free.**

The bag at the feet of the first man, **Alexander Darnes**: a medical bag. Darnes grew up in slavery, but after the Civil War (1861-1865) he finally got his freedom.

He went on to become the state's second African American physician and set up a practice in Jacksonville. Darnes was one of the most respected men in the city. When he died in 1894, around 3,000 people attended his funeral: more than any other in the city's history.

The second man wears a robe (like the kind people wear at graduations). **Edmund Kirby Smith** rose to the rank of general in the Civil War, then became a college professor. His great grand-daughter created this sculpture.

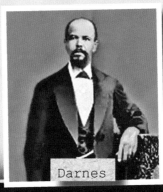
Darnes

Kirby-Smith

Time to test your image analysis skills once again.

☐ **TRACK DOWN THE HOUSE IN THIS 1800'S PHOTO.** **2** POINTS

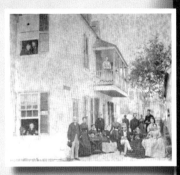

At the time of the photo, this building was a stylish inn/ boarding house, owned and operated by a...woman. Back then women weren't even allowed to vote, so owning a business was quite an accomplishment.

Avilés Street made an appearance in a 2004 movie, posing as a street in Peru, another former colony of Spain. Based on one of the best-selling books of all time, it follows a man hunting for a sacred text in the jungles of Peru.

☐ **WHAT WAS THE NAME OF THIS MOVIE?** **3** POINTS

For this intel, hunt down a plaque beside an old well - a well even older than the Castillo.

*Cofradia = a brotherhood devoted to a religious or charitable cause

☐ **LOCATE A SIGN WITH THIS SYMBOL.** **2** POINTS

Just after the Civil War, a group of eight nuns (from a sisterhood of nuns listed on the sign you found) ventured from their homeland of France to Florida to teach freed slaves. Behind this building stands their convent.

OLDEST HOUSE
AND ST. FRANCIS STREET

GONZALEZ-ALVAREZ
HOUSE
(THE OLDEST HOUSE)

☐ THE "OLDEST HOUSE" DATES FROM: CA. 17_7.

2 POINTS

(Ca = Circa; Circa = "approximately" when measuring a date)

Hint: Look for a brown bronze plaque.

Wood houses stood here before the date you just found, but they didn't stand the test of time or the flames of English raids.

☐ THE YEAR OF ONE OF THE ENGLISH RAIDS: 1 _ _ 2

2 POINTS

Find this sign for the answer.

A force of one thousand English troops attacked St. Augustine that year - battling for nearly two months.

15

- HOUSE YEAR
- RAID YEAR
- HOUSE FLAGS
- MILITARY GROUPS
- CAMINO REAL
- ST. FRANCIS

TOTAL POINTS

Thankfully, **St. Augustine's governor got advance notice of the attack.** He ordered all the townspeople into the Castillo to take cover and wait...and wait... and wait as their city burned outside. Finally their savior arrived on the horizon – Spanish warships from Cuba.

Examine the flags flying above the Oldest House.

☐ **WHICH FLAG(S) BELOW FLY FROM THE HOUSE?**

2 POINTS

Avilés, Spain

New Spain

Florida 1868-1900

Across the street find the plaque marking more remains of British attack. Today it's St. Francis Barracks - the HQ of two of Florida's military groups.

☐ **WHAT ARE THE NAMES OF THE MILITARY GROUPS?**

2 POINTS

The National Guard goes back to 1565 when a Spanish militia gathered to defend their settlement from enemy attack. Through the centuries, **one of the militia's most remarkable members, hands down: Francisco Menéndez.** Read on for his story...

You've heard of cats having nine lives, cheating death time and time again? Well, **FRANCISCO MENÉNDEZ** may well have had nine lives too. The below "intel" pieces together his life in the 1700's and reads like a movie.

Menéndez

Survives brutal journey from Africa chained to a slave ship, fed scraps, and surrounded by dead bodies

Risks his life to escape slavery in South Carolina

Fights alongside Native Americans in the wilderness

Captured and sold back into slavery in Spanish Florida, a land of free (and enslaved) Africans; Runaway slaves could get freedom if they became Catholic and fought in the military. While a slave in the city at first, he's finally free.

Leads our nation's first free black town: a military post outside St. Augustine, Fort Mose ("*Mo-zay*"); His new title: Captain Menéndez

Escapes death on the battlefield at the Battle of Bloody Mose; Protects St. Augustine and becomes a hero for defeating the British

Takes to the high seas as a Spanish pirate. A British crew captures him, learns that he lead Ft. Mose, and tortures him - enough to kill a man, but not Menéndez

Sold back into slavery in the Bahamas

Escapes slavery yet again and returns to St. Augustine

Sails off to Cuba in 1763 when the Brits take control of St. Augustine; Dies a free man in Cuba

Locate the "Camino Real" ("*Ka-mee-no Ray-al*") sign. Florida's first "highway" started as a Native American footpath, then grew to connect the Spanish missions. These spread Christianity to the natives and kept watch over Spanish territory. Nowadays it takes three hours to drive the route of the Camino Real.

☐ **BACK IN THE DAYS OF THE CAMINO, HOW LONG WOULD IT TAKE TO GO FROM ST. AUGUSTINE TO THE APALACHEE PROVINCE IN WINTER?**

2 POINTS

☐ **LOCATE THIS STATUE OF ST. FRANCIS.**
(from whom the chapel, missions, and barracks get their name)

3 POINTS

St. Francis of Assisi ("*Ah-see-see*") was born in the 1100's in Italy into a rich family and partied hard. He gave it all up to live as a poor man devoted to the Christian faith. **Francis was the first person to receive the "stigmata."**

One day, Francis witnessed a miraculous vision. When it ended, upon examining his hands, feet, and right side he discovered wounds. **They resembled the wounds of Jesus when he was bound to the cross and crucified.** The stigmata of Francis and others have mystified people for centuries.

St. Francis

(Francis helped treat people infected with leprosy, a disease which leaves marks on your skin. Some say the marks may have been from leprosy.)

☐ **EXAMINE THE HANDS OF THE ST. FRANCIS STATUE. WHAT'S YOUR TAKE - ANY SIGNS OF THE STIGMATA?**

2 POINTS

LIGHTNER MUSEUM SQUARE

Before you stands the old Hotel Alcázar (in Spanish Alcázar = castle) as well as a statue of Pedro Menéndez, St. Augustine's founder.

Carefully compare the real Menéndez statue to the statue's "doctored" photo above. Time for a test of your image analysis skills.

☐ **WHAT FIVE ITEMS WERE ADDED TO THE STATUE IN THE PHOTO WHICH DO NOT APPEAR ON THE REAL ONE?**

3 POINTS

25

TOTAL POINTS

Locate a statue sign with Braile dots.

☐ **WHAT DATE DID MENÉNDEZ FOUND ST. AUGUSTINE?**

2 POINTS

Menéndez was born and bred for the sea. He came from the port town of Avilés, on Spain's north coast where he battled French pirates. **He set off for Florida, looking for adventure, fortune...and to battle the French again.**

Menéndez left in July, 1565 with his massive flagship, the **900-ton** *San Pelayo*. (900 tons = two loaded up large airplanes) A month later (after a stop in Puerto Rico), he arrived off this coast. The date: the feast (festival) day of St. Augustine*.

Spanish ship replica

Then, on the date you found, **the crew of 800 came ashore and Menéndez established St. Augustine.**

*St. Augustine lived about 1,600 years ago in North Africa. He lead a wild life of sin, then changed his ways to become a priest, bishop, and finally a saint.

St. Augustine sees the light of truth

City Seal

☐ **FIND THE ROMAN NUMERALS ABOVE: MDCCCLXXXVI.** **3** POINTS

Roman numerals were the number system in Ancient Rome. Today, we find Roman numerals on clocks, monuments...and old hotels.

☐ **WHAT NUMBER IS THIS?** **3** POINTS

Use the below "decoder" for help. This was the year that millionaire Henry Flagler retired in St. Augustine. Flagler built the Alcazar, but in 1947 a man by the name of Otto Lightner bought it to display his fine art collection. (See "Lightner Museum" along with "City Hall" on the front?)

ROMAN NUMERAL DECODER

M = 1000
D = 500
C = 100
L = 50

X = 10
V = 5
I = 1

EXAMPLE:
MDCCLXXVI =
1776

Locate a sign that has the city seal (above), along with the city slogan, "_____ _____ City."

☐ **WHAT'S ST. AUGUSTINE'S SLOGAN?** **2** POINTS

Ponce

This slogan actually means: "St. Augustine - the oldest European city in the continental United States.*" **GOT ALL THAT?** That slogan is a mouthful- best to stick with the slogan in the clue you just completed.

☐ **TRACK DOWN A LION'S HEAD LIKE THE ONE ABOVE.**
   Ten Points Max

Hint: Walk around the corner of the building's entrance - and keep your head up.

Lions appear all over town:
1- The Bridge of Lions

2- A lion on the city seal

3- The Juan Ponce de León statue. In Spanish, León = Lion. (León is a region in Spain.)

☐ **BONUS: LOOK ACROSS THE STREET TO ANOTHER FORMER HOTEL, THE PONCE DE LEÓN (NOW FLAGLER COLLEGE), AND FIND ANOTHER LION'S HEAD.** **2 POINTS**

*The oldest city in the U.S. is San Juan, Puerto Rico, founded by the Spanish in the early 1500's. Puerto Rico is a U.S. territory. Of course, the Native Americans had large settlements long before Europeans ever came to these parts.

ZORAYDA CASTLE

Villa Zorayda, St. Augustine, Fla.

This building is modelled after an ancient palace in Spain, the Alhambra ("Ahl-ahm-brah"), minus, of course, the bright yellow, red, and blue paint.

Does the name Washington Irving ring a bell? Ever heard of *The Legend of Sleepy Hollow* and *Rip Van Winkle?*

The Alhambra

9

TOTAL POINTS

This author set off to Spain in the 1800's, made his way to the Alhambra, and fell in love with the exotic palace, leading him to write *Tales of the Alhambra*. One of the princesses in *Tales*: "Zorayda." In 1883 a millionaire from Boston (also enchanted by the mysterious Alhambra) built the villa, naming it after Irving's princess.

Irving

In the early 700's a group by the name of the "Moors," set sail to conquer Spain, ... making a quick trip across the sea •••••••••••••••• from North Africa.•••••••••••••••• (Spain's southern coast is only 9 miles from Africa at its closest point).

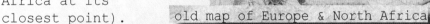

old map of Europe & North Africa

☐ **ACCORDING TO THE VILLA'S SIGN, HOW MANY CENTURIES DID THE MOORS RULE IN SPAIN?**

2 POINTS

A Moorish Court (right) in Spain

45

Boabdil

Ferdinand & Isabella

The Moors set up kingdoms across Spain. After ruling for hundreds of years, their final kingdom to fall was ruled by a sultan named "Boabdil," who lived in the Alhambra palace.

Boabdil surrendered his kingdom to King Ferdinand and Queen Isabella the same year the Moors were expelled (kicked out) from Spain.

☐ **WHAT WAS THE YEAR?**

2 POINTS

Surrender

46

Boabdil bids farewell to the Alhambra

This year may sound familiar. An explorer by the name of Christopher Columbus was at the Alhambra for this historic surrender.

Columbus

After getting the "thumbs up" from Ferdinand and Isabella at the Alhambra, he set off for the New World, in search of riches for the Spanish crown.

☐ **FIND THIS INSCRIPTION IN ARABIC, THE LANGUAGE OF THE MOORS.**

2 POINTS

It basically means, "There is no conqueror but God."

BONUS: Uncover the name of the Alhambra's city. (Scan a sign for this intel. It begins with "G.") Near the Villa, as you head back to the center of town, lies a street named after the city.

☐ **FIND A STREET SIGN WITH THE ALHAMBRA'S CITY NAME.**

3 POINTS

my notes:

FLAGLER COLLEGE

Henry Flagler

From King Street

Locate the statue of Henry Flagler, the "tycoon" for whom the college is named. "Tycoon" comes from a Japanese word "taikun," meaning "great lord." Flagler could've claimed that title in the late 1800's. He'd made millions with John D. Rockefeller (the world's first billionaire) through their oil empire – the Standard Oil company.

Rockefeller

Ever heard the phrase, **"If you build it they will come?"** In this case "it" was two things: Flagler's railroad that brought people down south to escape cold northern winters AND his three hotels that welcomed them: this one (called the Ponce de León) and the other two big buildings across King Street.

25

TOTAL POINTS

- FLAGLER'S RAILROAD
- ANIMALS
- HOTEL SIGN
- SPANISH SAYING
- EXPLORERS' NAMES
- BIENVENIDO SIGN

☐ **WHAT RAILWAY DID FLAGLER BUILD?**   **2 POINTS**

Hint: Read the statue's sign.

His railway still runs today, from Jacksonville all the way to Key West (but no longer carries travelers to fancy hotels).

VENTURE INSIDE THE COURTYARD AND FIND:

☐ **2 FISH**   **2 POINTS**

☐ **4 TURTLES**   **2 POINTS**

☐ **14 FROGS**   **2 POINTS**

SIA

49

☐ **THE OLD HOTEL NAME (PONCE DE LEÓN), IN LETTERS LIKE THIS:**

 2 POINTS

☐ **THIS SPANISH SAYING:**

 2 POINTS

NO SE HACEN TORTILLAS SIN ROMPER HUEVOS

Translation: "You can't make omelettes without breaking eggs." It basically means, "You have to sacrifice (give up something) to get something good." Note: In Spain "tortillas" are like omelettes (different than Mexican tortillas).

my notes:

_____

_____

Narváez   De Soto   a Timucuan
                                      chief

Make your way inside, under the letters of "Ponce
de León" that you just found. These remaining clues
inside the lobby building will truly test your
special agent abilities.

**FIND THE BELOW NAMES - IN LETTERS LIKE 'PONCE
DE LEÓN' ON PAGE 50. TWO POINTS EACH:**

2 POINTS EACH

☐ **NARVÁEZ:** ("*Nar-vah-ez*") Explored western Florida
in the 1520's

☐ **DE SOTO:** This Spaniard explored the Mississippi
River, the longest river in the U.S.

☐ **SELOY:** Chief of the Timucua, the Native American
tribe in St. Augustine when the Spanish came ashore
in 1565 (*"SELOY" will be in gold letters.)

☐ **PONCE DE LEÓN:** See his story on p.22.

☐ **RIBAULT:** (The "u" will look like a "v.") See his
story on p.8.

☐ **HUNT DOWN THE
'BIENVENIDO" SIGN.**

3 POINTS

(Bienvenido = "Welcome"
in Spanish)
(*"Be-yen-ven-ee-doe"*)

ST. GEORGE STREET

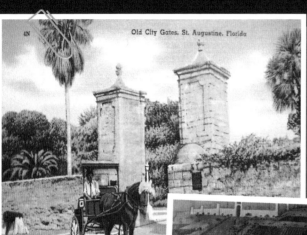

Old City Gates, St. Augustine, Florida

4N

The Oldest City in
The United States

The end of
St. George's
St. near the
Castillo

St. George's
Cross

AGENTS MUST HAVE A KEEN EYE FOR DETAIL.
THEY ALWAYS NEED TO HAVE THEIR EYES PEELED
FOR CRITICAL INFORMATION THAT OTHERS OFTEN
MISS. TIME TO PUT YOUR SKILLS TO THE TEST.

This street gets its name from St. George, the
patron saint of England, the legendary dragon
slayer, shown here saving a princess.

See his cape with the design of the cross of St.
George?

47

- BRITISH FLAG
- TABBY
- PEDRO CAMPS
- MINORCANS
- 1565 BRICKS
- TREASURY STREET
- MYSTERY SYMBOL
- JORGE BIASSOU
- WOODEN COVERINGS
- CITY GATE

TOTAL POINTS

In naming St. George Street in colonial days, of course it didn't hurt that **King George** ruled Britain.

> King George holding Emperor Napoleon in his hand. Napoleon (see p.19) was known for being short...but not that short.

☐ **WHILE EXPLORING THIS STREET, FIND A BRITISH FLAG (WITH ST. GEORGE'S CROSS) FLYING FROM A BUILDING. (SIX POINTS MAX)**

2 POINTS EACH

The Plaza divides St. George Street. For your first clue, venture to the quiet side of St. George Street (without all the shops).

Track down the remains of an old colonial wall – made of tabby (old-fashioned concrete).

☐ **TABBY IS MADE FROM THE SHELL OF WHAT ANIMAL?** **2** POINTS

> Hint: Find a plaque marking the wall's remains for this intel. You won't need to walk any further than Artillery Lane.

Cross the plaza to St. George Street's other side.

☐ **FIND THE STATUE OF THIS MAN, PEDRO CAMPS.**
2 POINTS

The people in this statue represent "Minorcans" (named after the Spanish island of Minorca). They left their homelands for Florida to work as indentured servants*, where their lives working a plantation (70 miles south of St. Augustine) took a turn for the worse. Many were either hungry, sick, or knocking on death's door. In 1777 hundreds ventured to St. Augustine to start anew. This man, their priest, led their struggle.

☐ **WHAT ARE THREE COUNTRIES THE WORKERS CAME FROM?**
2 POINTS

Hint: As you explore, keep a lookout for a sign with "Minorcan" in the title further down the street.

☐ **AS YOU WALK, FIND BRICKS WITH "EST 1565."**
1 point per brick, 10 points max
1 POINT EACH

☐ **POP QUIZ: WHAT DOES 1565 REPRESENT?**
1 POINT

*Indentured servants paid for their voyage from Europe to the New World by signing a contract to work for a certain amount of time after they arrived.

☐ **FIND THE NARROWEST STREET IN THE U.S., AND NAMESAKE OF THE ROYAL TREASURY.**

2 POINTS

Supposedly, Treasury Street was made just wide enough for two people, one on each side, to haul a chest. Gold would get unloaded from a ship at the port, hauled down Treasury Street, and deposited at the treasury. If the street was any wider, thieves in a horse-drawn carriage could sneak up and snatch the loot.

Before leaving town, make your way to where Treasury Street ends, just in front of the water, the site of these old images. ●●●●●●●●●●●●●●●●●●●●●●●●

☐ **HOW MANY TEAM MEMBERS CAN STAND, ARMS SPREAD, AT THE NARROWEST POINT?**

3 POINTS

(Return to St. George St. for the next clues.)

If you can complete the next clue, you truly have the keen eyes necessary for a special agent.

☐ **TRACK DOWN THIS SYMBOL ON THE OUTSIDE OF A BUILDING.**

5 POINTS

DON'T READ THE NEXT SENTENCE UNTIL YOU FIND IT.

This emblem marks the shrine of St. Photios ("*Fo-tee-ose*"), dedicated to the first Greeks who came to the U.S. from your earlier clue.

Biassou

United States — Miami — The Bahamas

Key West

Havana

Cuba — Turks & Caicos

Camagüey

Santiago de Cuba

Cayman Islands

Jamaica

Haiti — Port-au-Prince

Santiago

Santo Domingo

Dominican Republic

Puerto Rico — San Juan

Atlantic Ocean

Caribbean Sea

☐ **FIND THE BUILDING ONCE HOME TO THE COUNTRY'S FIRST BLACK GENERAL, JORGE BIASSOU.**

 2 POINTS

(Jorge Biassou = "*Hoar-hay Bee-ah-soo*")
Read the home's sign for the next pieces of intel.

☐ **BIASSOU CAME HERE AFTER LEADING THE SLAVE REVOLT ON WHICH FRENCH ISLAND?**

2 POINTS

By 1791, the French slaves of this island had enough of their brutal masters and sought revenge and freedom. Biassou came to command a force of 40,000 ex-slaves in this uprising. Spain controlled the other side of the island. Looking to bring down their French rivals, the Spanish armed ex-slaves like Biassou, gave them money, and Spanish citizenship for their fight. Soon Biassou set off for St. Augustine (controlled by Spain), where the arrival of his larger-than-life character drew the attention as if you saw a celebrity walking down St. George Street today.

☐ **HOW MANY PEOPLE WERE IN HIS "ENTOURAGE?"**

2 POINTS

☐ **WHICH FORT DID HE LEAD IN ST. AUGUSTINE?**

2 POINTS

He had a salary second to that only of the governor. Upon his death he had a lavish ceremony fit for a general. Nowadays, he's even made it into the "Assassin's Creed" game, quite an honor indeed.

Track down an anchor and chain hanging from the side of a house.

☐ **HAVE YOUR PHOTO SNAPPED WITH THE ANCHOR.**

2
POINTS

Before you stands the Oldest Wooden Schoolhouse, built in the early 1700's. The anchor and chain didn't arrive until 1937 - to hold the old schoolhouse in place in the event of a hurricane. So far so good.

☐ **LOCATE A WOODEN COVERING LIKE THIS.**

1
POINT
EACH

Guards once posted here in the 1800's, sizing up all who passed through St. Augustine's northern boundary.

☐ **TAKE A PHOTO OF YOUR CASE OFFICER(S) AT THE CITY GATE.**

2
POINTS

my notes:

ANYTIME MISSIONS

THE BEST AGENTS HAVE A HIGH LEVEL OF SOMETHING CALLED "SITUATIONAL AWARENESS." ("SA" FOR SHORT.) THESE QUICK-WITTED AGENTS PAY CLOSE ATTENTION TO THEIR SURROUNDINGS – READY TO COLLECT CRITICAL INTELLIGENCE AND RESPOND TO DANGEROUS SITUATIONS.

These clues will test your SA. Don't let your guard down as you wander around, or you'll miss a chance to win points.

TWO POINTS FOR EACH OF THESE SPOTTED:

☐ **HORSE DRAWN CARRIAGE *WITH* PASSENGERS** 10 points max

☐ **TOURIST TRAIN/TROLLEY *WITH* PASSENGERS** 10 points max

☐ **PERSON WEARING OLD-FASHIONED CLOTHES** 10 points max

☐ **FLORIDA'S SEAL ON A SIGN**

(a Seminole woman with hibiscus flowers looking towards the sun and a steamboat)

20 points max

FOUR POINTS FOR FINDING SIGNS OF EACH OF THESE STREETS (NAMED AFTER SPANISH CITIES):

4 POINTS PER STREET

☐ **SEVILLA** (*"Seh-vee-ah"*)

Spain's treasure ships left from Sevilla to sail to the New World to load up on loot. In St. Augustine (one of the loaded ships' "pit stops" before the return to Spain), pirates stalked the vessels, hoping to seize the treasure. If the loot made it back to Spain, it would get unloaded in...

☐ **CÁDIZ** (*"Kah-deez"*)

One of Ponce de León's most important discoveries: the Gulf Stream. This ocean current whisked treasure ships back to Cádiz in record time. Pirates attacked this port too, including the famous "Dragon" (p.11).

☐ **CORDOVA** (a.k.a. "Córdoba" in Spain) ☐ **VALENCIA**

☐ **THREE POINTS FOR EACH BUILDING WHERE AT LEAST TWO OF THESE FLAGS FLY TOGETHER** 15 points max

3 PTS PER BUILDING

(The designs of the middle flags may appear a bit different, but the colors will be the same.)

St. Augustine's Rule

1565-1763:
Spanish

1763-1784:
British

1784-1821:
Spanish

1821-NOW:
U.S.

ANSWER KEY FOR QUESTION CLUES

Once an answer is submitted, your case officer can check it here. If you peek at this answer key before submitting a final answer, you won't receive any points for that clue.

#1 Visitor Center/ Correct order of the masks: F-C-D-E-B-A; Sister city name: Avilés; Item given to the Sister City - an anchor. The Old Spanish Trail ended in San Diego. St. Augustine's Spanish name - San Agustín. City residents went to the island of Cuba. The disease - yellow fever.

#4 Plaza de la Constitución/ The document the men signed: the Declaration of Independence; Ponce's arrival: 1513. The U.S. acquired Florida in 1819; Florida became a state in 1845. The state song - "Old Folks at Home." "The 'March to the Plaza'" was June 9, 1964. The three people who spoke the three quotes: Andrew Young, Jr., Martin Luther King, Jr., Lyndon B. Johnson. The latitude/longitude numbers: 29 degrees North, 81 degrees West.

#5 Government House/ The building's function: post office. The king and queen's names: Juan Carlos and Sofia. The stars in the flag: 34. The boundary: west.

#6 Avilés Street/ The street's old name: Street of the Royal Hospital. The house in the photo: Ximenez-Fatio House. The movie 'The Celestine Prophecy.'

#7 Oldest House/ It dates from circa 1727. The year of one of the English raids: 1702. The flag: New Spain. The names of the military groups: Florida National Guard, Military Department (State of Florida). The Camino trip length in winter: four days.

#8 Lightner Museum/ Added to statue: Cross near the sword handle, cloth piece on his right shoulder, two pieces of cloth on upper thighs, metal "dot" on the cross on his chest; He founded St. Augustine on Sept. 8, 1565. The Roman numerals: 1886. The city slogan, "Nation's Oldest City."

#9 Zorayda Castle/ The number of centuries on the sign: six. The year: 1492. The Alhambra's city name: Granada

#10 Flagler College/ He built the Florida East Coast Railway.

#11 St. George Street/ Tabby is made from oyster shells. The three countries: Greece, Spain, Italy. 1565 = St. Augustine's founding. Biassou led the revolt on Haiti/St. Domingue. His entourage: 26 people. He commanded Ft. Matanzas.

THE FINAL MISSION

Completed *Mission St. Augustine*? Congratulations!
Visit **www.ScavengerHuntAdventures.com** with your
case officer.

☐ GO TO "**SPECIAL AGENT CERTIFICATES**"
TO RECEIVE YOUR VERY OWN OFFICIAL
CERTIFICATE.

SIA

☐ PICK UP YOUR FREE COPY OF OUR
E-BOOK, **THE MUSEUM SPY**.

Put your sleuth skills to the
test as you analyze clues in
world-famous pieces of art.
Be sure to sign up for our
newsletter, the "**INSIDER**," to
become the first to know about our latest
mission destinations.

THE MUSEUM SPY
BROUGHT TO YOU BY SCAVENGER HUNT ADVENTURES

GREAT FOR GROUP TRIPS!

We offer **special multi-copy pricing** and **personalized
books** - great for field trips and group vacations.
Email us at **info@ScavengerHuntAdventures.com** for
more info.

MISSION DESTINATIONS
Paris, London, Amsterdam, Rome, New York, Barcelona,
Washington, D.C., and St. Augustine - more missions on
the way.

IMAGE CREDITS: Images supplied by the author or from www.bigstock.com are not listed. Cover images are taken from book interior pages. They are credited by book page number. Images from Wikimedia Commons, Flickr Commons, and the Florida Memory Project are below. The two digit numbers are the file license number (links below), links to Flickr photographer sites are also below. License for all Flickr photos is Creative Commons 2.0. (T=Top, B=Bottom, M=Middle; L=Left, R=Right, C=Center) WIKIMEDIA: p.5-British Library-3.0; p.6:T-Library of Congress-3.0; p.7:B-The Natural History of Carolina, Florida and Bahamas-3.0; p.8:M-British Library-3.0;B-National Park Service-3.0p.11:B-National Maritime Museum-3.0; p.12:M-Kunsthistorisches Museum-3.0; p.13:B-Ningyou-3.0;p.14:M-New York Public Library-3.0; p.15:T-Smithsonian Museum of American Art-3.0; p.16:TR-www.bassenge.com;B-Sailko-3.0; p.17:T- Author Mainstreetmark-3.0;B-Jonathan Zander; p.18:R-National Archives-3.0; p.19:T-National Gallery of Art;M-Ayuntamiento de Sevilla;B- Francisco Macias Library of Congress; p.20:Library of Congress-3.0; p.22:TM-British Library-3.0;TR-National Archives-3.0; p.23-M-National Portrait Gallery-3.0; p.24-B-National Archives-3.0; p.25: TL-Library of Congress-3.0;TR-Lyndon Baines Johnson Library and Museum-3.0; p.26-T-U.S. Navy-3.0;BL-www.korea.net-3.0;BR-Heralder-3.0; p.27-T- Ssolbergj-3.0; p.29:T-Eigenes Werk-2.5;M-FDV-3.0; p.30: TL-Daniel78-3.0;TR-Library of Congress-3.0;M-National Archives-3.0; p.31:TL-Dept of Defense;TR-Library of Congress-3.0;p.34 TR&TC-Heralder-3.0;BL-www.jaxhistory.com; p.37: L-Ningyou;M-Mikel Gonzalez;p.38:St. Augustine 450th Commemoration;p.39:T-Mdhennessey-3.0;B-Santa Croce-3.0; p.41:B-LA County Museum of Art; p.42-TL-Heralder-3.0;p.43-TR-British Library-3.0; p.44-B-Slaunger-3.0; p.45-T-Library of Congress;M-Berkeley.edu; p.46-TR- Avila Madrigal de las Altas Torres;B- Die Welt an der Schwelle zur Neuzeit; p.47-T-Toledo Museum of Art;M-Cristobal Colon.Net; p.48-M-Library of Congress-3.0;p.50-TL-Noroton-3.0; p.51-TM-Historichair-3.0;TR-www.openlibrary.org-3.0; p.52-L-Musée Jacquemart André; p.53-T-Metropolitan Museum of Art-3.0; p.56:TL-Juan López Cancelada-3.0; TR-Kmusser;B-IntergalacticZ9-3.0; p.59-Museo de America Madrid-3.0; FLICKR: Note: Boston Public Library = BPL; p.4:T-BPL; p.7:TL-Michael Seljos; p.10:ML-Yakin669; p.13:T-BPL;M-Sandy Auriene Sullivan; p.14:T-Dan Lundberg;p.15:M-James Jones; p.18:L-BPL; p.22-B-BPL; p.27-B-Free Stock CA; p.28:BPL; p.29- Junta Informa; p.31-TC-John Schanlaub; p.40:L-Dan Lundberg; p.41:M-Moultrie Creek; p.44:T-BPL; p.48-TL-H. Michael Miley; p.52:TL-BPL; p.55-TL&TR-BPL;B-Ted; p.58-T-BPL; LINKS TO FLICKR PHOTOGRAPHERS; Example: https://www.flickr.com/photos/boston_public_library/ = boston_public_library/; Boston Public Library: boston_public_library/; Centrilobular: centrilobular; Cliff: 28567825@N03/4439634192; Dan Lundberg: 9508280@N07/; Emanuel H: ensh/; Florida State Archives: army_arch/; James Jones: puggles/; John Schanlaub: 32011723@N03/3714711371/; Junta Informa: juntainforma/; Korea.net: koreanet/14758513027/; Michael Miley: mike_miley/; Michael Seljos: 99149846@N00/; Moultrie Creek: moultriecreek/; Nic McPhee: 26406919@N00/2575830297/; Peter Long: peterlong/; Ted: frted/; Yakin669: yakin669/5365576357/in/set-72157625752020703/; FLORIDA MEMORY PROJECT: p.12:T;p.32: Baptista Boazio, Saint Augustine Map, 1589, Collection M81-21; www.floridamemory.com/exhibits/floridahighlights/mapstaug/; p.35: State Archives of Florida, http://floridamemory.com/items/show/8042 (Retrieved from Wikimedia: p.11:T&M; p.51: TL: State Archives of Florida (no link given)); Links to Licenses:1.0: http://creativecommons.org/licenses/by-sa/1.0/deed.en; 1.2: creativecommons.org/licenses/by-sa/1.2/deed.en; 1.5: creativecommons.org/licenses/by-sa/1.5/deed.en;2.0: creativecommons.org/licenses/by-sa/2.0/deed.en; 2.5: creativecommons.org/licenses/by-sa/2.5/deed.en; 3.0: creativecommons.org/licenses/by-sa/3.0/deed.en INFORMATION SOURCES: City of St. Augustine historical markers; Associated Press. "Anchor From Shipwreck Makes Trip Back to Spain."; Bjorkman, Sue. "Haunted happenings provide different perspective on history at St. Augustine Lighthouse." St. Augustine Record; "Castillo San Marcos" The St. Augustine Record; Donges, Patrick. "50 Years Of The Civil Rights Act: Dr. Robert B. Hayling." WJCT News.; Edwards, Virginia. 'Stories of Old St. Augustine.' Hawk, Robert. "William Wing Loring: Florida Militia to Egyptian Pasha." Florida Dept of Military Affairs; http://www.melfisher.org/1622.htm; Jacinto, Anton. "The Constitution that never was." El Pais newspaper; Jacksonville Historical Society. "Alexander Darnes: Jacksonville's First Black Physician."; Lewis, Ken. "For The St. Augustine Four, civil rights war began with order for burger." The Florida Times-Union.; Macias, Francisco. "Banner Proclaiming the Spanish Constitution of 1812." Library of Congress Blog.; Marx, Robert; Marx, Jennifer; 'Treasure Lost at Sea: Diving to the World's Great Shipwrecks.'; Meide, Chuck. "The Loss of the French Fleet and the End of French Florida." NOAA Ocean Explorer.; National Park Service. "Castillo San Marcos."; Parker, Susan. "Nation's Oldest City: St. Augustine survived English seige in 1702." St. Augustine Record.; Robison, Jim. "Myths Cling To Legend Of Osceola." The Orlando Sentinel.; "Tapestry: The Cultural Threads of First America." City of St. Augustine. Turner, Sam. "Ponce de León's Discovery Timeline." St. Augustine Record.

SPECIAL THANKS TO NICOLETTE NORDAN,'TOUR ST. AUGUSTINE' GUIDE!

Made in the USA
Columbia, SC
11 November 2017